Vox Publica:
Poetical Works

William Graham
2007

Text © William Graham 2007.

All rights reserved. No part of this book may be reproduced in any form or by any means, electronic or mechanical, including photocopying, recording or any information retrieval system, without prior permission in writing from the publishers.

ISBN-10: 1-4196-6823-4
EAN13: 978-1-4196-6823-4

Interior formatting/cover design by
Rend Graphics 2007
www.rendgraphics.com

Published by:
BookSurge Publishing, LLC.
www.booksurge.com

To order additional copies, please visit:
www.amazon.com

To an Impassioned Interest in Interpreting Life

☜☞

Sonnets

1

Dawn's dreary light creeps through the trailer park
Casting cold light on dirty used cars
That cough and rattle in the waning dark.
Dogs yelp, straining their chains, as men with scars
And caps pulled tight over wary eyes
Depart through barren fields frozen with fists
Of black dirt. Men try to forget the cries
Of their children who each day must resist
The temptation to strike back against taunts
Made by Nordic locals who do not hide
Their contempt for dark amigos who haunt
The schools, churches and stores where they reside.
  Men rub rough, sore hands that will rip the guts
  From butchered chickens until the sun sets.

2

Dirty towels lie scattered on the floor
Of the elegant bathroom, still fragrant
From the tropical shampoo much adored
By women whose heels clack on dry pavement.
Bending down to scrub the toilet, she felt
A volcanic pain erupt in her back.
Her moans struck the tiles; she thought she would melt,
Convinced that her body was under attack.
She sat on the edge of the king-size bed,
Covers thrown to the side, pillows stained
With the guest's carmen make-up that bled
Into the cotton threads like a slit vein.
   She noticed cash on the cream bedside stand;
   Two ones, she sighed, crushing them in her hand.

3

How many feet have been cut and bloodied
Walking on the sharp lava that once poured
From the mouth of Mauna Kea to the sea?
Countless weary travelers have scored
The black stones to announce to those who walk
Behind them that shelter from the cool rain
Is near. Amidst the storm, elders talk
Of gods who roam the tropical terrain,
Ruling the island with pomp and power.
The islanders have vanished from the trails;
Sounds of children's choral cries from the hour
Of dawn now swallowed by the trade wind's wails.
  As the clouds creep to Mauna Kea's red peak,
    They drip tears of ancients—no more to speak.

4

We must reach the summit of Mauna Kea
Before sunset. The bus trudges up slopes
Like a mountain climber gasping for air.
Darkness pours into the valley. Our hopes
For a sweet sacramental sunset soar
As the bus unloads our fellow pilgrims
At the top of Hawaii. Look lower--
Clouds swirl like debutantes as the day dims.
Mauna Kea casts its last sultry shadow.
Tropical sun leaves with a diva's flair.
The evening's astral troop takes a bow
As they enter the vaulted stage. We stare
  At their gleaming performance. We ignite
  With joy at the clarity of the night.

5

Another withering dawn greeted her
As she placed calloused feet on the rug
That was a gift from Grandmother Sawyer.
Yawning, she poured coffee into the mug
From the floating riverboat casino
Where she and her sister Irma gambled
Fifty dollars each Saturday to show
Each other that their lives could not be bled
Dry of every luscious childhood dream
Of caressing excitement like a lover.
She attacked her sagging blank face with cream;
Lurking mortality now covered.
  On the bus, she sat devoutly silent;
  Singly anonymous, she came and went.

6

The sun opened the lid on his bleak skull
And poured in equal measures exhaustion
And regret as he pushed tar to the wall
That surrounded the high house of fashion,
Perched smugly on a hill with a lake view.
Wiping the trickling sweat from his worn eyes,
He thought of the tall woman he once knew
As his smart bride, now diminished in size.
She now slumps, sighs and sobs in a wheelchair,
Staring at the kids playing in the park,
Awaiting his return to stroke her hair,
Pleading with him to hold her in the dark.
   She would like this house, he thought. Cool lake air
   Sliding across her skin, massaging despair.

7

She watched him leave the house with a scarf
Wrapped too tight across his face and his hood
So secure that the other boys will laugh.
Quieting his protests, he understood
Grudgingly that she did not want his face
To freeze in the sarcastic wind that whipped
The ash trees like horses starting a race.
He avoided the branch on which he tripped
Yesterday as he ran beside the road
Where snow drifts like dirty sheets have piled
Up against rotting fences. She had told
Him to ignore boys' taunts; then she smiled.
   Through the steamed windows of the old bus
    He saw the only person he could truly trust.

8

The cold night sky slit open and gave birth
To a trembling sliver of green light.
Pulsating with newborn joy above the earth,
The light arched its back and spun with delight.
Stunned travelers looked to the heavens
And saw a sinuous green harp take shape,
Ghost strings wildly plucked by unseen hands send
Shocks to their skulls; they plan their quick escape
From the ice-blasted plateau to the snug
Warmth of their reindeer bags. They dare not gaze
Long at the rolling arcs of light; they hug
And speak of the dead whose souls are now raised.
   For these are blood lights-souls of warriors
   Battling, sparks flying from glowing spears.

9

The geometrical man glided to
The office like an elegant theorem,
Confident that his grand proofs would subdue
The skeptical flock poised to disprove him.
He launched into his cool, crisp oration
Like a Greek mentor delivering lessons
To pupils, who deferred confrontation.
Perched passively like sparrows on a fence,
They absorbed the bleak clarity of words
That hung in the room like condemned traitors.
Arms crossed, pens scratching aimlessly, they heard
Formulas to lead them to the right course.
   His neat axioms meant no jobs for some;
   For him, mere academic abstraction.

10

Placing his thick leather hand on his cane,
He shuffles gingerly to the fireplace,
Slowly scanning trophies that would remain
His salvation, shrines to muscular grace
That has now been swallowed by the hole
Of diminishment—sequoia stature
Felled by time and disease. His lofty role
In the house ravaged by faulty nature.
Green passions have changed to autumnal brown,
The hue of empty fields covered with frost.
All the past eloquent joy has now grown
Into arid memories—often lost.
   Sitting back down in his favorite chair spawns
   Thoughts of a life with consequence, not yawns.

11

Three boys with unruly hair charge up a hill
On an empty public golf course looking
For a mountain of leaves that will
Serve as their outpost for the day. Leaves cling
To their sweaters as they plunge and tunnel
Into the crunching tower of color.
An apple-cheeked boy emerges; he fumbles
For his glasses, but they are not anywhere.
Panicked, he enlists his friends to assist
Him in finding the precious spectacles.
Frantic, afraid, the boy cannot resist
The urge to sob for being so reckless.
   No glasses are found. The boy slowly strides
   Down the hill to where punishment resides.

12

Brian and I push away the branches
That choke the muddy path to the quarry.
We had heard the rumor of caves that his
Older brother had told. Jimmy's story
Was that robbers used the damp, cold caverns
To hide money and other treasures stolen
In daring stick-ups. Such a grand tale burns
Our imaginations. We are driven
To search for the legendary riches
Like conquistadors slogging through the swamps
Of the new world. A quick halt and Brian says
There's a cave behind the rubble. He stomps
   Through brown mud puddles. I follow. Then we cheer
   Briefly, for the cache is just smokes and beer.

13

Their breath floats like angels in a fresco,
Swirling around heads wrapped against the cold
Of a January day at five below zero.
Lavender ladies arrive to behold
The glory of God in the drafty church.
Wooden pews give scant comfort to old bones.
Crooked parishioners rub hands and search
The church, reporting the gossip in hushed tones.
"In the old country, you would never see
Men in jeans; such a disgrace to our Lord."
"And that young woman there, she now has three
Yelping children on her hands; oh, my word."
  Mass starts; a rattle rises from the chest
    Of an old man; he wipes phlegm from his vest.

14

She sits in the hot, cramped seminar room
Dreaming of sleek boardroom belladonnas
Whose arpeggio careers she would soon
Emulate. Looking around, she would pause
Her racing thoughts to wonder if the men
Sitting across the shiny table know
She contains virtuosic opinions
Like a corporate impresario.
One semester remains before her grand
Debut in the marketplace. Already
She has booked her vacation in the sand.
From her quaint, modest condo she must flee.
  A life of stature she must assemble;
  Corner office queen she must resemble.

15

The morning sun lights the black brick manor
Like a theater spotlight. Brightness rules
On a day when most people gathered there
Expected to find black water in pools.
Old friends and questionable relations
Enter the front hall parlor. Mourners mill
About like penguins, recite quotations
Of condolences and then remain still—
Dry hands fold in front; heads bend in respect.
The family begins their procession
Past the coffin. Aging children inspect
The matriarch with cold introspection.
   Her last demanding breath unlocked their chains;
   They can now savor the life that remains.

16

The old brown pickup sputtered to life
Like a coughing invalid. Widow Joan
Pulled herself in the cab for the drive
To Orchard Junction. Not reared to bemoan
Her lonely state, she went resolutely
About her daily affairs with the same
Natural cycle as an apple tree.
Turning at Route 1, she refused to blame
The Lord for taking Max on a Friday
Afternoon when he was pruning the trees.
Still warm under a Macintosh he lay.
She neared the town and thought of groceries
   For her grandchildren—eleven and eight.
   The boy looked like Max—sturdy, tall and straight.

17

He hopped on his gold Schwinn for the ride
Down the hill and through serpentine streets.
He fled from the war zone. He could not abide
Persistent salvos caused by the defeats
Of the previous evening's skirmish.
He raced past lawns refreshed by morning dew.
Turning the corner at Fourth Street, he wished
To vanish in a corner to pursue
His dream of floating down the Amazon
In a rusty boat with old Gustavo.
Silent ladies checked in books placed upon
A Homeric desk. He knew where to go
   Without asking. He climbed black iron stairs;
   Finding the chair of quiet adventures.

18

Like a jungle cat I crouch in the thick
Bushes—poised, breathing muffled, a ball of
Potential energy. There, a quick
Rustle of leaves. A skittish bird above
Me exits with a sarcastic farewell.
I focus on the small meadow in front
Of me. If my hot prey is not careful,
The grass will be its Gettysburg. My blunt
Disregard for my opponent's feelings
Is crucial to my hunting persona.
My cautious combatant mockingly clings
To the meadow's far margin. I choose the
   Truest arrow from my plastic quiver.
   My prey hops once; then dies with a shiver.

19

At least once a year we made the journey
Through verdant farm fields that undulated
Like politicians' positions—a sea
Of corn and alfalfa cultivated
By farmers wearing grubby green Deere hats
And sporting three-day beards and dirty nails.
The gravel road spat rocks at our car. Flats
And thick heat were part of the trip's travails.
Aunt Carrie lived life alone in Cascade
In a grim upstairs apartment over
Hank's Hardware Store. For our visit, she laid
Out cake and poured lemonade. A cover
  Of ancient dust clung to the furniture.
  I was told that a smile I must conjure.

20

The brown stains from numerous summer rains
Looked like tears on the peeling green siding
At Uncle Albert's house. Rusting remains
Of a lawnmower provided the hiding
Place for a solitary gray rabbit.
As we entered his house, the aroma
Of beer and unwashed overalls drifted
To our noses. He put a robe on
And sat on the edge of a sagging bed
Jammed against the livingroom's stark white walls.
Local updates in machine-gun brogue sped
From his mouth like bullets. A housefly crawled
   Around the rim of a bottle of Hamm's.
   But the smell of rotting food changed his plans.

21

The rusting pickup truck pulled a trailer
Bulging with elephantine lawnmowers,
Trimmers and plastic bins. Dawn's early glare
Bored into the men's eyes. One trimmed near stairs
While another mowed the model lawn.
Six in the morning; fourteen hours to go.
The men left old Mexico for the long
Journey north with strong wills and backs. They stowed
Their money in the worn heels of their boots.
They lived faithfully in an apartment
With six other compadres. Sunday suits
Hung crisply—worn to take the sacrament.
   The sun attacked them; nowhere a shadow.
   Eight in the morning and twelve hours to go.

22

The air is as still as a sleeping child.
Nature holds its breath. Dirty green clouds
Smudge the treetops. Birds cease singing. All wild
Creatures hunker down as deep darkness shrouds
The neighborhood. The grandmother next door
Shuffles outside on crooked legs to pull
Her laundry off the line as a loud roar
Shatters the silence, shaking the steeple
Of the church like an angry heretic.
Mothers up and down the street beckon their
Children to stop playing baseball and get
Back into the house, as the sirens blare.
   Lances of lightning duel in the heavens.
   Wind whips through windows and assaults curtains.

23

She could resist everything except
Temptation. This is what she jokingly
Would tell herself as lonely anguish leapt
From her mind and chardonnay flowed freely
Into her throat. With her two young children
Dropped off at grandma's, she sat with her feet
Propped on the sofa, thinking of the sin
Of wishing she could just hide and retreat
To a secret Shangri-la where marriage
Before nineteen, two kids before twenty-two,
Divorce before thirty and cold rage
Before noon were actions she would not do.
   Fifty dollars tucked in her mail-order purse;
    The Blackhawk Casino would drown her curse.

24

Every time I enter another
Country has joined the United Nations
Of hair cutting. On my inaugural
Visit, I was led to the work station
Of a maternal Russian whose husband
Suffered from sciatica. Rita cut
Hair dreaming of dipping toes in the sand
Of a Caribbean isle. Etiquette
Dictated that I respond politely,
Telling her that Aruba in the winter
Must be heaven. One day, I did not see
Her. Clippers and combs gone; swiveling chair
  Now turned by a nymph from Estonia
  Who loves couture and drives a Toyota.

25

Where did the people go who used to live
In the white clapboard house? Their rich black fields
Now lie frozen and fallow. Who will give
The tilting barn with the words "Jesus Heals"
Written on its side a fresh coat of paint,
A helping hand to make it stand upright?
No volunteers are raising hands at Saint
Patrick's cemetery. Many polite
Regrets arise from the deep, cool chambers.
"No thank you. We did our chores a long time
Ago. Every soul here remembers
The long days that made us old in our prime."
   "We sired and reared many ruddy boys.
   But they are gone. They made other choices."

26

The tree stood like an old man, crooked
And weathered, in a dense forest behind
Our house. A century old, it was said.
Grand and mythical, we could never find
A more holy tree in which to construct
Our sanctuary from parental laws.
Using sturdy planks that we could abduct
From our fathers' caches, we gathered nails, saws,
Hammers and screws. The oldest was foreman.
I was part of the small construction crew.
We nailed wood in a fever with no plan.
Thick boards creaked and strained as a strong wind blew
  Through branches that cradled our fortress.
  Dialogue within—we would not confess.

27

The director placed the politician
Carefully in the green rural tableau.
"We must show John in the right position."
"The cornfield as frame is the way to go."
Today, Saville Row was not the best choice.
John grabbed instead a faded red plaid shirt,
Blue jeans and boots—the ensemble to voice
The concerns of voters whose hands touched dirt.
But for John, milking cows, felling old trees
And planting corn were from times long ago.
He reaped the riches of commodities.
Fortune made, he was prepared to bestow
   His platinum opinions on the state:
     "God and people's rights we must venerate."

28

The call came to her cell phone as she went
To pick up four-year-old Allie from school.
"Don has been hurt at work. He has been sent
Straight to Angels of Mercy hospital."
She dropped off Allie at a neighbor's house.
Don had caught the pre-dawn train from Fox Lake
With his construction buddies Phil and Mouse,
Who met her with a slow, silent head shake.
Yellow hard hats in hand, they parted
As she entered the antiseptic room.
She saw his boots on the floor. She started
To cry. She knew that sorrow would consume
  Her. Phil and Mouse expressed condolences.
  They returned to work to take their chances.

29

The short night before I had carefully
Placed my broken-in glove by the backdoor.
Crickets sang to me as I waited to see
The first spike of dawn stab the wooden floor.
I pulled off the gray tarp that covered
My gold Stingray, protecting it from dew.
I slide my glove on the handle and sped
Up the street, heading for Field Number Two.
When I arrived there was already a pile
Of bikes lying like metal spaghetti.
We were instructed to jog single file
From home to center at two-fifty-three.
   The hot air sizzled on the sun's griddle
   As I vacuumed balls hit up the middle.

30

Sister Constance asked us all to write down
Our sins neatly on a piece of paper.
We should memorize each transgression known
To live in our hearts in its darkened lair.
Swearing and disobeying our parents
Were the sins of choice for this fresh-faced crowd.
In our green pants and white shirts, we were sent
Down the street to church—no talking allowed.
Ushered into the painful wooden pew,
I cranked my head up to investigate
The vaulted ceiling, thinking of the view
From the highest rib, from where God could take
   In the solemn show. I kneeled; closed the door.
   Penance: two "Hail Mary's"; one "Our Father."

31

Everyday they see the detritus
Of the town. They are traveling voyeurs
Who peep, prod and probe—not to frighten us
But to serve. For them, it is de rigueur.
They are a muscular trio riding
In their growling metal truck redolent
Of the rotting food that each week we bring
From the store and don't eat. But the coin spent.
Don't think they don't make snap judgments. They do.
"That's a perfectly good leather lounge chair."
"Look at these nice suits. The young mother threw
Them out. Hubby scooted with the au pair."
   Next house—for three bottles of smooth whiskey
   They help a widow with a fallen tree.

32

Early morning fog hovers like a ghost
O'er the moist grass behind Saint Mary's church
In the Lake District. Hills there have been host
To many a shy, rambling poet in search
Of the raw spark of imagination.
A man of many worn years ambles slowly
Up the path to Pine Rigg. His elation
Over the vistas unfolding at every
Turn is tempered by the knowledge that life
Is sarcastically seeping from his shell.
He stops at Loughrigg Terrace—a view rife
With poetic grandeur. He hopes to tell
   His grandchildren that while still on this earth
   He will seek out great words that have true worth.

33

There was a soft knock on the classroom door
At about eleven in the morning.
A disembodied hand beckoned Miss Moore
To the hall, interrupting our boring
Lesson about geometrical blocks.
Miss Moore called my name. Zach Frost muttered
Something rude and began to wildly mock
The way I walked. In the hall, I stuttered
When asking if I had done something wrong.
My teacher and another tall woman
Had moist eyes—the kind Mom got when a song
About love played. They told me what happened.
   Sister dead. Then somber chaos; long tears.
   A box four feet—one for each of her years.

34

Unshaven men slumped over cups of coffee
Like dry ferns drooping for lack of water.
Heads felt like sandbags used on a levee.
Except for the occasional slow stir
Of the spoon through the murky brew, the men
Sat silently. They turned their heads like owls
When someone entered their stainless steel den.
Each trucker was a night creature who prowls
His territory. From Durham to Denver,
Racine to Roanoke, they rumbled through
Dreary industrial parks to drop their
Loads and pick up another. No one knew
  Their names. One man's last gulps sloshed in his throat.
  Mortgage to pay. Five hours to Terre Haute.

35

I'm standing here sipping chablis from Chile,
Surrounded by a pile of corpses who
Talk about missing the great symphony
Last Saturday because of the zoo,
And the children, the traffic and fatigue.
When did they stop being interesting?
What day did they jettison their intrigue
For life besides their daughter's ice skating?
They used to be my friends. We used to talk
Of sunning like lizards on exotic
Beaches. Now, when adventure calls, they balk.
Water parks are now their life aquatic.
   I am forty. I don't want to submerge
    My life for kids. Do not yet play that dirge.

36

Perched on a high bluff like a brick vulture,
Her house peers down on the small river town,
Where, for eighty years, she has lived a pure
And simple life—nary a care or frown.
Her livingroom ceiling drips like the nose
Of a child. Sierras of newspapers
Weave through the narrow halls piled with old clothes.
Skunks have set up house under the porch stairs.
A family of confident raccoons
Dresses in the attic for a wild night
Of garbage prospecting under the moon.
Mice scurry from the walls for a quick bite.
   The woman decides to dress to the nines—
   A grand meal with cutlery that still shines.

37

Even wrapped with red and green paper, I
Knew what the long, thin box under the tree
Contained—my telescope. The country sky
Would yield its celestial secrets to me.
On Christmas Eve, I feigned gleeful surprise
When I ripped the wrapping off the package.
Leaving undistinguished gifts for sunrise,
I donned winter gear and tramped to the edge
Of the frozen cornfield behind our house.
Galileo-intense, with the tripod
Forced securely in the hard snow, I crouched,
Tilted the lend up, and let out a loud
   Gasp as the shimmering lunar surface
   Assaulted my eyes and made my heart race.

38

The sharp shards of cracked glass in his head lanced
His brain. Confusion oozed like battle wounds.
One moment tuned to Bach; the next he danced
Like a dervish and made mad howling sounds.
His wife shuffled their children to their rooms
When Tahiti was replaced by Hades.
Through closed doors, they heard how panic consumed
Their mother as she searched for razor blades.
When all was quiet, the quivering kids
Poked their red, tear-stained faces through a crack
In their doors and crept slow with chrysalis
Emotions to the kitchen bathed in black.
   Their father lay in a blue sleeping bag.
   Mother wiped food from the floor with a rag.

39

John thought he had been dreaming when the phone
Rang loud at two o'clock in the morning.
He groaned as cold room air flooded the zone
Of warmth under the comforter. The springs
And his forty-something bones creaked as he
Groped for the phone hidden on the nightstand.
His groggy wife Joan turned over to see
What was going on. John reached for her hand.
Their son Brian had been in a car crash.
"But that is not possible. He's in bed,"
Joan cried as she sprung from bed in a flash
Of panic and ran down the hall with dread.
   He was not there. Their car had disappeared.
   Three boys dead. Blunt force trauma. Rooftop sheared.

40

I could sleep all I wanted to and suck
My thumb to my heart's content in the womb.
One moist, muggy day I had the bad luck
To be pulled to the rough light. Who dared presume
I would prefer to be wrapped like a sausage?
Who had the audacity to believe
I would consider it a privilege
To hear harsh incomprehensible squawks
Assaulting my delicate ears each day?
I guess the service is satisfactory,
But I must respectfully request play
Time with a dash more creativity.
   I pledge to cradle you in your dotage.
   But show me the world; show me you're a sage.

41

From the hard streets of the Dominican
They come to play. From the twister-lashed fields
Of Oklahoma, where the horizon
Is cruel, they come to hit and rack up steals.
Young, tall and smoldering with ambition,
They come by car and bus. No airport here.
Duffle bags plop down at the Red Roof Inn.
Players pray and coaches look for a beer
To discuss the blank slabs they must chisel
Into steady hitting, pitching Greek gods.
"That Caribbean kid's heater whistles
By everyone. He might just beat the odds."
   A rookie stares into the empty park.
   Crickets sing as his dreams float in the dark.

42

Sister Constance implored us to wear gloves,
Hats and boots for the twenty-minute walk
Up the hill to the college perched above
The town. Drivers would honk loudly and gawk
At our bundled troop keeping pace through snow
Drifts and up steep, ice-slicked sidewalks that rose
To the red-brick campus, where the star show
Was about to commence. We shed our clothes
And sat down in the planetarium.
We swam in the huge chairs that tilted back.
This was a field trip for learning, not fun,
We were warned. Eyes adjusted to the lack
  Of light. Then the high ceiling exploded
  With stars. Had we witnessed the sacred?

43

The only creatures awake are a stray
Cat and me. I bound out of bed when dawn
Pulls back the curtains in my room. Today
I must start before the competition.
I drop bland cereal down my gullet
And head to the thick jungle that cradles
The fairways of Bunker Hill Golf Course. Jets
Of water soak greens. Thoughts of parables
About early birds and tortoises fill
My head with inspiration as I slog
Slowly through tangled brush that tests my will
To find elusive lost golf balls. I log
   Twenty trophies for my cache. Now I wait,
   Look for a fair price and grow my estate.

44

Lines of limousines disgorged elegant
Ladies and gentlemen who dripped panache.
Couples hovered like divine angels sent
From heaven. The marble hall was awash
In new jewels and old money glances.
The grand opera's first act had begun
Before the music had played. Finances
Were discretely discussed. Homes near ski runs
Were compared to compounds in Grand Haven.
A financier counseled an attorney
On offshore investments as his raven-
Haired fourth wife's youth glistened like a marquee.
   Many were impressed with the scenery;
     Others preferred snoozing to Puccini.

45

When Father Roy wore his faded plaid shirt,
He was off duty at the rectory.
When not saving souls, he liked to assert
He was more than just a monsignore.
He was reared in rural Wisconsin with
The pigs, chickens and cows on a small farm
Where God and his mother dealt with the filth
Of heart and body. His limber right arm
Was his salvation from the burly boys
Who would otherwise have abused him for
His saintliness. Pinpoint control and poise
On the hill caused his sinful soul to soar.
   But God wanted more than a wicked curve.
   Roy retired his old mitt when called to serve.

46

I was always feline meticulous
With my music. Every rehearsal
Had to be precise or it was a loss.
I struggled with my bandmates, who would sprawl
On stained sofas, looking like Civil War
Casualties—hirsute, grotesque, silent—
Medicated with whiskey by the jar
Or the latest crop from the Orient.
Yet I whipped them into being rock stars.
There were cataracts of legal tender,
Passionate red tongues and Cuban cigars.
But brief was the raw fame and the splendor.
   In my neat Maine home, I wrap black tape
   On the tailpipe. My next gig—to escape.

47

The neighbors expressed shock to the news crews
That descended like flies to the cul-de-sac.
No mother could believe that such abuse
Lurked in the tranquil house where, in the back,
A geometric flower garden grew.
"It was like a miniature Versailles,"
A woman explained, as a silk wind blew
The yellow police tape. "Such acts defy
Comprehension," another said softly.
But there were secrets in the faux chateau;
Terrors that the older children would see
And not reveal—a mother would explode
   At a fair toddler's disobedience.
   Insanity would be her best defense.

48
In Memory of Harrison Hayford

Books tumbled down from shelves like glacial scree.
Discolored paper peaks rose from the floor.
He pointed to a poster: "Do you see
What it says?" His soft laugh slid to a roar
That shook the tall leaded windows. "Starring
In the title role is Gregory Peck!"
The movie was *Moby-Dick*. I was learning
The dry humor of the man from a speck
In rural Maine. Cows, barns and dirty snow
Were exchanged for the quads of Yale College.
There, he found his life's work. He came to know
Melville like a brother. A privilege
  It was for me to hear him weave his tales.
    Call him Harry—scholar and a friend to whales!

49

I often think about obstetricians.
They see tears of joy on people's faces.
But I see only grief. Morticians
Like me must perform the work that erases
The last remnants of warm life from the earth.
We clean up when the party is over.
I have to ask: "How much is the life worth?"
A simple question of math. But it can stir
The flames of resentment in survivors.
I gently remind them that the final
Exit shapes lasting memories. Flowers,
Music, casket—they are symbols to all
   Who will assemble to whisper farewell.
   Even with death, it's knowing how to sell.

50

He had his secluded studio built
In the woods behind the house that had been
The grand stage for many dramas of guilt
And retribution for generations.
While his wife socialized with the ladies
Of the lake, he would struggle in the chill
Of autumn to stay out of the Hades
Reserved for writers who have lost of thrill
Of finding the *mot juste*. Now be scribbled
Aimlessly, looking for a theme worthy
Of his past stature, as field mice nibbled
At aborted manuscripts. He could see
   The sun tugging at the sky. He remained
   At his darkened desk—slumped, as his mind strained.

Verse Variations

Blond Ambition

Born the first daughter to a gray flannel
Man and a woman who favored Chanel,
Darling Claudia, with hair of fine gold,
Slid into the world, never to be cold.
Father would take the train into town,
Leaving Mother and Claudia to crown
Each other queen and princess of the house.
Claudia was never allowed to grouse
About her ensemble. Pretty dresses,
Sparkling shoes and ribbons in her tresses
Were always in fashion for a daughter
Of her social stature. Parents bought her
All that was required for a safe, royal
Life in the suburbs. No trauma would spoil
Her life on Green Street. Even when dear Father
Lost his job at fifty, a trust fund steered
Them clear of ruin. He then spent his days
Reading the *Times* and sipping cabernets.

Mother was a fixture at the school board,
Pushing for fresh paint and gardens restored.
"Children must be surrounded by beauty.
How else can they find truth? It's our duty."
Claudia found that school was quite charming.
She wrote for magazines; bought the class ring.
After she was graduated with much pomp
And circumstance, she jetted to the Champs-
Élysées—la plus belle avenue du monde.
Voila! A wealthy French lawyer she found.
He had perfect family connections.
She fell in love. He hid indiscretions.

Her parents told her to cease and desist.
The match was improper for a Methodist.
Claudia returned to start her college
Career at Smith. She sadly acknowledged
That the Frenchman had to go. Deceiving
Men she would avoid. She started achieving
What was expected of a Smith woman.
She studied and flirted with lesbians
Chastely. On one wild night, she had to spurn
A girl's passionate kisses. Lesson learned.

After two years, she missed her native ground.
With the tame and proper she surrounded
Herself. She returned to her leafy town.
At Lake Forest, she earned her cap and gown.
She had no inclination to look for
Employment. Like Mother, she was more
Interested in social volunteering,
Which meant planning events and being seen.
She attended church services on Sundays
To find a spouse. Mysterious are God's ways.
An engineer from a family firm
Caught her blue eyes. Ivy League she would learn.
She bedded him quickly. His endowment
With hers would be joined in a permanent
Union sanctified by the holy church.

After the Parisian honeymoon, their search
For a large house ended admirably
In a cul-de-sac with dignified trees.
One son arrived and then two blond daughters.
She was consoled by their joyful laughter;
For she was often alone. Maintaining

Their estate and possessions was draining
The life out of her husband. Her Mother
Chided her, saying: "There is no other
Place you would rather be. Don't expect more.
This house, this life; it's what you most adore."
That said, they sat and drank Chilean wine
While sharing one *Royalty* magazine.

Vermont Morning

Wife and child remained asleep as the sun
Trudged over Vermont's long spine—the Green Mountains.
The jungle room of night opened its door
To the morning regulars—the odor
Of freshly barbered grass, the satisfied
Sounds of sheep filling their bellies. Eyes wide,
Pole in hand, solid canine by my side,
I began my regular morning trek
Up the mountain. Our homestead became a speck
In the chilled valley. At the bare summit—
High Peaks glowing in the west—I would sit
And imbibe sweet silence. This is why
We escaped the urban chaos—the sky
At dawn, vistas deliciously untamed
By misguided sprawl. In the years that remain,
We will grow gray watching our beloved boy
Smell tall cedars—touched by natural joy.

Encounter on Mount Washington

She sat like a stone sentinel.
Her intense stare at Tuckerman Ravine
Disturbed my pleasant trek. I heard her tell
The chilled air that she would never be seen

Again. Then she began rocking like
A hobby horse as she wrapped her thin arms
Around her waist. Should I disrupt my hike?
Would she return home? Or do herself harm?

I continued ascending the steep trail.
Clouds lowered and hard rain began to drill
Into my jacket. The wind howled like male
Artic wolves. I decided that the thrill

Of reaching the peak must wait. I plodded
Downward. I did not observe the woman.
Her high, craggy perch was empty. I searched
The newspaper the next day. My slow scan

Yielded no mention of any missing
Hikers. One my next attempt to ascend
Mount Washington, with the north wind hissing
Like angry opera fans badly offended,

I tried to comprehend my chance meeting,
But decided after fruitless review
That the odds are small of unraveling
Secrets of one who wants to say adieu.

Adirondacks

Manhattan blue-bloods used to travel here
To take the cure, to escape the fetid
Urban air. In their lakeside homes they hid
From the rustic locals' knowing hard sneers.

The glorious Adirondack peaks soared
Above the blue expanse of Lake Champlain
Like granite sentinels. As a spring rain
Dripped slowly and thunder began to roar,

A curtain of dirty clouds descended.
I stood on the narrow ridge of Mount Abe.
The gloom soon lifted; the setting sun made
A double rainbow, lightly suspended

Over the lake, framing the jagged peaks.
The tame view from a grand holiday home
Cannot compare to this—the sublime tome
Of nature. Higher ground is what I seek.

Croagh Patrick

There is a locomotive
In my chest as I scramble
Like a goat—but not nearly
As nimble—up the gray face
Of saintly old Croagh Patrick.

Rain—chilled like a fine chablis—
Sarcastically spits at
Me from the November sky.
I am alone except for an
Old man who dashes past me
Like a dimly remembered
Dream—the kind you are not sure
Is real or just a shadow.

As my ankles twist in the
Loose rock, I pause to catch my
Breath and stare at Clew Bay and
The green hills that lie beyond.

I wonder if Saint Patrick
Stopped at this same windy spot
To drink in the lovely view,
Or if he only looked up
At the summit where he would
Fast for forty days alone.

I wonder if the thousands
Of pilgrims who march like ants
Up the slope on Reek Sunday—
Many climbing on bare feet—

Can see the beauty as they
Wipe the caked blood and the mud
From their cracked soles before they
Recite seven "Our Fathers,"
One "Hail Mary" and one "Apostles' Creed."

I drink water and nibble
On a baguette and sharp cheese.
My eyes stray from the steep path
To see clouds breaking over
County Mayo like a grand
Sacrament. I am satisfied.

Mont Blanc

Shelley told me that Mont Blanc "gleams on high."
But romantic poets have been known to
Garnish. I went to Chamonix to view
For myself the peak that pierces the sky.

A woman with no teeth and an eye patch
Bid me in mumbled French to follow her
To my Spartan room. A "Merci, monsieur,"
And she left, closing the door's rusty latch.

Through my crusted, cracked window I could see
Mont Blanc casting its imperial shadow
On the verdant valley floor far below.
Its cold countenance dripped serenity.

Days I stayed to savor its solitudes;
To drink in the Alpine forests and streams.
Shelley's poem of primeval power still gleams.
In the vales, evening's languid fog broods.

Iceland

The giant hirsute raiders from Norway
Were primed for a fight as they rowed ashore.
Did they find monks? Or was that Celtic lore?
From long boats they surveyed the steaming bay.

They called it Iceland—so the sagas tell.
They settled in narrow, hidden valleys,
Reared horses, built homes from scarce trees.
They avoided the hidden people who dwelled

Beside them. Families fought and settled
Old scores from the old land. Generations
Were bred and buried in isolation.
Blood and lava flowed the same—hot and red.

Volcanoes still rumble; the earth still splits.
But today's Icelanders are civilized.
Genetically the most pure—the prize
Won by living on an island that sits

Under the midnight sun. Now men named Rolf
Only use clubs during a round of golf.

Newfoundland

A moose lazily trots through
A gas station in Rocky Harbour.
For locals, it is nothing much ado.
But I stop pumping and stare.

With my car fueled, I drive
To Lobster Cove Lighthouse for the ten o'clock sunset.
Aromas of pine and salty seas arrive
As the sapphire sky melts into russet.

The Vikings might have decided not to stay,
But the moose and I enjoy the display.

Mount Kosciuszko

Some scoff at the notion of calling you
A mountain worth hiking, Mount Kosciuszko.
Your dome has endured dismissive glances
From the hiking cognoscenti. Stances
Like theirs do not stop me from coming here
During the antipodean summer
To scale your rocky bump above Thredbo.
Morning fog shrouds your summit. I forego
The lift and take the long twisting ascent
Through alpine forest and heath. My Yank accent
Is a curiosity for many
I pass in the mist. Aussie antennae
Can still detect a stranger in their midst
Even if many of the blokes are pissed.
On the peak, a stranger throws me a look:
"Bloody boring, mate. Kiwi's have Mount Cook."

Machu Picchu

My heart rattled its cage like a jungle
Cat in the liquid blue Andean air
As I willed my burning legs up the stairs
Placed in the mountains by the Incas. Still

Bleeding from tickets sharp as razors
That intertwined like passionate tongues,
And with little oxygen in my lungs,
I emerged in the temple of condors.

I walked the geometrical terraces
And gazed at the rumbling Urubamba
Deep below. I touched Intihuatana
Stone with my forehead and tasted the stars.

Rapa Nui

Petrified stone heads gaze at the waves
From a lava speck in the southern sea.
Faces of Rapa Nui royalty.
Their carvers lie in anonymous graves.

Did their labor mean anything to them
As they chiseled to dusk?   Their bleeding hands
Shaped silent, immortal countenances.
Their faces to obscurity are condemned.

The curious cross the sea to unravel
Forgotten builders' final syllables.

Oxford

A vernal warmth crept on cat's feet
Through the quadrangles of Oxford.
Ancient church bells' angelic chords
Told people in the narrow streets

The time. I did not see scholars
Rushing on cobblestones, with their
Long black robes flapping in the air,
Looking like giant crows. Mahler's

Kindertotenlieder floated
Poignantly from a practice room
Window; its elaborate gloom
Echoed on gray stone walls coated

With centuries of British grime.
Poets, preachers, philosophers
And rogues have climbed rutted stairs
To reach tutorials on time.

These towering spires and meadows
Lush have sent the world grand ideas
And bright policies to free us
From darkness with their thoughtful glow.

I strolled past the many colleges—
Home to studious fellows all.
Do their sublime thoughts still enthrall?
Or now stone dead is such knowledge?

Mortality

When he looked in the bathroom mirror,
He avoided the temptation to stare.
What he saw was a cheap horror film
Projected on his face. He would skim

The obituaries in the past;
Now, he studied them closely over breakfast.
A college friend dropped dead at sixty
Running in a race for charity.

His wife was a photo on the wall.
One day, he feared, he would not recall
Her voice. On item was his comfort—
Her bathrobe hanging in the closet.

He could still see her in the red silk—
Thighs smooth and the color of warm milk.

The Quiet Man

The lawn service arrived every week
To cut his grass. His neighbors were happy.
No alarm was raised when they failed to see
Him around. His absence was not unique.

Spirited baseball games were played across
The street in a city park. Long balls flew
To his yard. Players scaled his fence and threw
The dingers back. Autumn came; leaves were tossed

Against his silent house. Winter's snowdrifts
Piled on his porch. They say he had been dead
Since spring. A phone call from a cousin led
Police to his house. A stroke—death was swift.

Country Graveyard

Elderly trees planted as windbreaks bend
Like faithful celebrants at Sunday mass.
The oaks' robust leaves protect the grass
From the sun's barbaric rays that descend

From the prairie sky. A random pick-up
Will fly by tossing dust on the gravestones.
Infants, widows, war heroes all have bones
Planted in the glacial soil. With any luck

An aging relative will come to pull
Weeds from their plot. The last priest from Divine
Word church died. The parish will never find
A new disciple to preach the Gospel.

Soon, no one will be left to visit here;
Leaving all to bees searching for nectar.

Lost

A face that I once saw everyday
Is gone. Not dead, but absent in her own way.
Does she live between Mumbai and Calais?

Her voice has dimmed; laughter gone mute.
I remember her sorrow was so acute.
She played guitar, or was it the flute?

She talked of travel to the south of France—
Renting a villa and finding romance.
She studied Zen yoga, or was it dance?

She dreamed of having three fine children.
I heard this did not come true. Bad choice of men.
I wondered if she cried or said "Amen?"

Her calls have stopped. Postcards do not come.
I do not know to what she has succumbed.
She preferred red apples, or was it plums?

Insurgents

I see them arrogantly
Scurry along electrical wires
Like furry gymnasts from
The rodent Olympics.

I see them sniff diligently
At the grass in my manicured
Lawn, desperately trying
To find something on which to gnaw.

I see them methodically
Dig in the dirt with their
Maniacal miniature
Claws, leaving scarred earth behind.

I see them chase each other
Around tree trunks at a hundred
Miles an hour defending their
Territory—which is really mine.

I see them delightfully
Gorge themselves on my
Devious concoction of
Peanut butter and poison.

Now I no longer see them
Strut like generals in my
Yard. Controlling insurgents
Requires harsh tactics. Mission accomplished.

Tyranny of Choice

I just need one new pair of socks.
But I am confronted with two hundred pairs staring at me
Like stray animals in a shelter looking for a home.
I just want to know who won the election.
But I must wade through an Amazonian thicket of channels
and sites.
With all of these selections and inventions,
Why can't most Americans find our nation's
Capitol on a map?

To Jackson at Four

Now that you can talk and express opinions;
Now that you can conjure alternative realities on your own;
Now that you can fly a kite shaped like a dragon and
Ask probing questions about the wind, stars, sun and moon
Worthy of the ancient Incas,
It's time I tell you that it's my job to
Teach you how to think, not what to think.
You are never too young to celebrate Independence Day.
That's one truth I hope you will find self evident.

690388

Made in the USA